Minimalism

How to De-Junk and Downsize Your Life

Colvin Tonya Nyakundi

Simple Life Books

Mendon Cottage Books

JD-Biz Publishing

Disclaimer

The information in this book is provided for informational purposes only and it is not intended for use as a substitute for proper financial or legal direction by a qualified financial or legal advisor. The information is believed to be accurate as presented based on research by the author.

No claims of income are given and examples are used to portray the ideas of the author as possibilities without representing actual earnings that can be made.

The author or publisher is not responsible for financial loss or damage incurred by implementing ideas mentioned in this book. The author or publisher is not responsible for errors or omissions that may exist.

Warning

The Book is for informational purposes only and before starting or running any business, it is recommended that you consult with your financial or legal professional. Always follow all laws and regulations regarding taxes, selling, buying, or ecommerce.

Check out some of the other Entrepreneur Series books
Entrepreneur Series books on Amazon
Check out some of the Science of Living Series books
Science of Living Series on Amazon
Check out some of the Health Learning Series books
Health Learning Series on Amazon

Table of Contents

Introduction

Are you overwhelmed with what is going on in your life? Maybe you're hearing these endless noises in your mind and you don't know how to overcome them. Are you always busy to the extent that you can't find time for yourself or for those closest to you? Is your home full of junk? Well, you're not the only person having these problems.

Millions of people from around the world have so much junk in their lives. According to research by renowned institutions and scientists, most people don't need and never use about 80% of the stuff that they own. Apart from the junk in their homes, they keep on buying and accumulating more stuff each day. If you're interested in getting rid of these junk, you have to downsize and minimize your life.

Downsizing may involve moving to a smaller house, getting rid of some of the property that you own or changing your lifestyle. When downsizing, you have to change your daily routine and find new hobbies.

The book "Minimalism: How to De-Junk and Downsize Your Life" is equipped with strategies on how to minimize the stuff in your home, how to move to a smaller house and how to cope with less stuff. Once you read this book, you'll also learn about what you must never miss in your home when downsizing.

This book is also designed to help all those who're interested in downsizing and minimizing their digital files. You should therefore read this book if you want to downsize the files in your computer(s) or phone.

Your lifestyle will be completely changed once you downsize and de-junk it. This means that you might be affected emotionally or psychologically. However, you have nothing to worry about because this book is equipped with tips on how to cope with your new situation.

All those interested in joining the military should read this book because it will equip them with skills on how to downsize their life. Even if you're not planning to join the military, you must read this book because you'll learn important life skills on how to survive with little stuff.

Why You Need to De- Junk and Downsize Your Life

(well maintained and clean small summer lodge)

Have you ever walked into a compound that was so clean and organized that you wished it was yours? Did you litter the place? According to research, people are less likely to litter clean environments than dirty ones. The only way your home can be clean and organized is if you de-junk and downsize it. With such a home, you can be sure that nobody will litter the place.

According to scientists from around the world, people living in cleaner and more organized homes are calmer and less stressed. This means that they're less likely to suffer from conditions such as paranoia, depression, anxiety and underperformance. You can therefore improve your quality of life and live healthily by simply de-junking and downsizing your life.

When downsizing by moving to a smaller house, you'll reduce your monthly mortgage repayments. This means that you'll save more money and hence secure your future. Even if you decide to buy the house with your savings, it will be much cheaper than a larger home.

By downsizing your life, you'll spend less money on utility bills including electricity, water and natural gas. Think of it this way; a smaller house will have fewer bedrooms and hence fewer bulbs are required to illuminate the entire home. With reduced number of bulbs, you'll definitely pay less electricity bill. During winter, you'll require less energy to heat the entire house. You'll also use less water to clean the house and irrigate the flowers and vegetation surrounding it.

How many servants do you currently have? How long does it take you to clean the entire house? With a smaller home, you won't have to hire several house helps. If you decide to do your house chores, you'll take less time. This is because the surface area to be cleaned is much less and hence requires fewer hands and less time. With a downsized house, you're guaranteed that the home will always be clean because you won't ever forget to clean a section of the home. This means that you'll be more comfortable to invite your friends over for drinks or dinner.

It is also much cheaper to maintain a smaller home than to maintain a larger one. You'll use less paint on the walls and fewer pieces of pipes to replace the plumbing system. Since outdoor flowers and vegetation will be reduced, you'll require less manpower to trim them.

An average American spends more than 30 minutes each day searching for something that they've misplaced and probably won't easily find. You therefore have to consider minimizing and downsizing your life if you never want to misplace anything within your home. It is much easier to manage a smaller house and locate something instantly. Even if you kid is playing with the TV remote control, you won't have to worry about anything because there is no way that he/she can misplace it.

When compared to a very large home, a smaller property is more secure and hard to be invaded by burglars. This is because it is harder to hide in a smaller house than in a larger one. In case somebody breaks into your home in the middle of the night, you'll immediately detect it. It is also quite difficult for any wild animal or reptile to hide inside your home without being detected. In case there is something missing in your house, you'll immediately notice it if you live in a smaller one. Therefore, you should downsize your life by moving to a smaller house if you want to improve your personal security and safeguard your property.

(when living in a smaller house you won't feel the loneliness that you normally feel when in a large and empty living room)

How do you feel when you've just entered a large and empty room? Do you feel lonely and isolated? Well, with a smaller house, you won't ever feel loneliness. This is because the house will always be full and hence you won't feel the emptiness in your life.

It is also quite easy to replenish the stuff in a small house than that in a larger one. Normally, a large house consists of so many things that you'll feel lazy to go replenish the consumables. On the other hand, you'll immediately replace the consumables in a smaller house since it won't require much energy or effort.

Apart from moving into a smaller house, you also have to consider minimizing the number of activities you're involved in on a daily basis. This way you won't have many commitments and hence you'll have more time to yourself and to spend with family and friends.

Moving into a Smaller House

(a small house with a small front yard)

Moving into a smaller house is one of the hardest things that anybody can ever do. It is even harder if you've lived in your current home for a very long period of time. This is because you'll probably be so used to your current house and everything in there. Actually some people are so used to the stuff in their homes that they can't stay away for even a week. Regardless of all these, you have to move into a smaller house if you're interested in minimalism, de-junking and downsizing your life.

The world is a very dynamic place and hence it is quite difficult to predict the future. For example, you might get fired without notice and hence be forced to move into a smaller house. You can also be transferred into an area in which there is no large and spacious house.

If you're thinking of joining the military, then you have to learn how to live in a smaller house, anywhere in the world under any conditions.

In your quest to de-junk and downsize your life, you should not move into a house in your current neighborhood. This is because you'll feel too bad, driving past your old house each day and remembering how big and spacious it was. The only way you can overcome your emotional attachment to the larger house is by moving to a different neighborhood.

While it is important to expand your investments, you don't have to occupy two homes at the same time especially if they're within the same locality. So as to downsize your life, you have to sell or lease out one of the homes. You'll get some extra money while at the same time downsizing your life.

How many members are there in your household? Do you live with your spouse and one child? Before you move into a new home, you have to consider the number of people in your household. This will help you decide the maximum number of bedrooms that should be in your new home. For instance, if you live with your spouse and one kid, you just need a house with three bedrooms: one bedroom for you and your spouse, the other one for your kid and the spare one for guests.

So as to minimize and downsize your life, you can move into a room with a smaller study room. If you have so many books, just sell or donate the ones that you've already read. The only books that you need to retain are those that you'll need in future. For instance, you should retain your professional books because you might refer to them in future. You can also modify your new study room to accommodate more books. For example, you can increase the height of the shelves and hence accommodate more books.

Unless you're moving to the countryside, you shouldn't move into a home with a very large backyard. The larger the backyard the more the money you'll use in maintaining it. This means that you can never downsize your life by moving to a home with an expansive backyard.

(you don't need a gazebo when there are several trees near your home)

Why do you need to construct a gazebo/summerhouse yet there are several trees surrounding your home? So as to minimize your life, you should learn to use what you already have instead of accumulating more stuff. For instance, you can spend your summer afternoons under the tree next to your home instead of constructing a gazebo.

You also don't need a room with too many bathrooms. An average person spends less than ten minutes in the shower each day. If there are four people in your household, you can decide to move to a house with just two bathrooms. You'll share the two bathrooms between the four of you. By sharing the bathrooms, you're also likely to reduce your water consumption since you'll be spending less time in the shower.

The size and shape of your living room should be considered before moving into a smaller house. You don't have to move out of a large living room only to settle in another house with a similar living room. If the property in your current home can't fit into your new living room, just sell or donate some of it. Before moving into your new home, you can seek the services of an interior decorating expert to help you optimally utilize the available space.

How many people can your sofa set and dining room table accommodate? If you live with your spouse and kid, why do you have a seven-seat sofa set? So as to minimize your life, you have to consider selling your current sofa set and purchasing a smaller one.

Some people buy a new television set without bothering to dispose the old one. If you have more than one television set, then you need to consider selling them and retaining only one. This is because the TVs are occupying so much space and hence making your house look too congested. If you've kept one of the TVs in the bedroom, just sell it and use the one in the living room.

Throughout your life, you should never own more than one car at the same time. However, this doesn't mean that you can't buy an automobile for your spouse. A household of three members should have a maximum of three cars at any given point. If you have extra ones, donate or sell them to your other family members or friends. So as to completely downsize your life, you can also decide to sell your current car and buy a new smaller one.

Unless you're running a home based business, you don't need supercomputers or extra-powerful computers. Normal, readily available computers are small, cheap and can serve anybody efficiently. If you have several powerful computers whose abilities you never utilize to the maximum, you probably have to sell them and replace them with less powerful ones.

(you have to get rid of all those t-shirts that you never wear)

You probably have several t-shirts in your bottom most drawers. You were most likely given the t-shirts when attending events. Perhaps they have labels and logos publicizing the event that you attended. Since you know very well that you won't ever wear these t-shirts, why are you still keeping them? Why don't you give them away?

In your quest to minimize your life, you shouldn't forget to downsize the kitchen. To get started, note down the type and quantity of each item in the kitchen. These include the number of knives, saucepans, serving-spoon, bowls etc. Since you won't ever use more than one knife at the same time, why are you having so many of them? So as to downsize your life, you have to consider disposing the extra kitchenware. You can also move into a home with a smaller kitchen.

You don't need a very large kitchen and too many utensils if you know that you don't like cooking.

After visiting several friends or places, you've probably collected numerous gifts, memorabilia and souvenirs. So as to de-junk your life, you have to get rid of some of these collectibles. Start with the ones that remind you of bad events. You can then go ahead and dispose those that don't remind you of anything important.

Downsizing Your Lifestyle

Apart from moving to a smaller house and de-junking your home, you also have to minimize your activities. Downsizing your life is all about making sure that your life is as simple as possible.

(unsubscribe from some of your membership clubs)

To begin with, you have to reduce the number of membership clubs in which you're subscribed to. You don't have to be a member in all clubs in your area. So as to downsize your life, consider unsubscribing from some of the golf and country clubs, football associations and hockey clubs. Keep in mind that it is not possible to be in two places at the same time. You should therefore retain only the clubs that you frequent. After unsubscribing from the memberships, you should find alternatives to your hobbies. If you're used to spending too much time on the golf club, you can now start spending your time with friends and family.

You don't need to subscribe to the gym for extra hours than you need. Don't subscribe for two hours per day when you know very well that you can only work out for a few minutes before getting tired. Minimize your life by reducing the number of hours you're subscribed to the gym each day.

How many classes/lessons are you currently registered to? Some people are registered to so many classes including swimming, ballet, singing and dancing. You can simplify and downsize your life by simply de-registering from some of these classes. You should take one class at a time.

How many TV channels are you currently subscribed to? How many hours do you spend watching TV each day? If you're subscribed to several TV channels, you have to get rid of some of them and retain only the ones that broadcast your favorite shows, movies and series. Apart from saving some money, you'll also save some time since you won't be spending too much time in front of the TV.

Due to the flexibility and convenience of online movies, more and more people are subscribing to movie streaming websites instead of the traditional broadcast television. Through streaming websites any movie, series or show can be watched on demand. So as to downsize your life, you have to consider unsubscribing from some of the websites in which you're a subscriber. You can also decide to go for pay-per-view movies instead of monthly subscription. This way you'll be sure that you're only paying for the content that you watch.

You probably don't need high speed internet connection if you never watch or download online movies. Unlike slower internet connection, high speed connectivity is quite expensive and may require special and expensive equipment. Light browsing can be achieved through low speed internet connectivity. If you want to downsize your life, talk to your internet service provider (ISP) and ask the company to provide slower but cheaper internet connectivity.

How many trips or safaris do you undertake each year? Where do you normally go during your holidays? Unless you're super-rich, you don't have to go on holiday or safari every now and then. Downsize your life by reducing the number of trips that you undertake each year. You can also explore local tourist destinations instead of visiting distant places.

(reduce your smoking and drinking rate)

You must stop your 'bad habits' if you want to downsize your life. For instance, you can reduce the number of cigarettes that you smoke each day. You can also reduce your alcohol consumption. If you're too much addicted to the internet or movies, then you need to do something about it. If you find it hard to stop your 'bad habits,' you should seek professional help.

How many cars have you owned in the past five years? If you're thinking of minimalism and downsizing your life, you must stop frequently replacing the property that you own. You don't have to change your car, TV, phone or even furniture yearly.

You don't need too many clothes and pairs of shoes. At any given moment, you can only wear one set of clothes. You can simplify your life and live more comfortably by simply ensuring that you never own so many pieces of clothing at the same time. To minimize your life, dispose some of the belts, suits, pairs of shoes and socks, shirts, pants or blazers that you own.

When downsizing and de-junking your life, you should never forget to do something about your digital life. You can start by getting rid of all those DVDs and CDs that you never watch or listen to. Donate or sell the DVDs and CDs that you've already watched.

You should also get rid of all the junk/unimportant files in your computer. You can decide to do it manually or use software that aids in computer cleanup. Go through each of the files and folders in your computer. If you haven't opened a given folder or file in the past six months, you probably don't need it. You should therefore delete it immediately.

When downsizing your digital life, you can decide to store or backup your files online. Keep in mind that you can always conveniently access your online files from any device at any time of the day in any location around the world.

When minimizing your digital life, you have to be very cautious about the software that you install in your computer. If you're not careful, you can easily install malware or spyware. You should also avoid installation of different software doing the same task. For instance, you don't need two media players in your computer. Install one with the many features and a friendly user interface.

To begin the process of downsizing your lifestyle, buy two diaries. In one diary, note down every place you visit each day and what you do while there. Also note if the place or event makes you happier than usual. In the other diary, list all your expenses. Even if the money is deducted directly from your bank account, you should list the expense in this diary. Do this for at least three months. If you notice that you've paid or you've been charged some money consistently for a given subscription while you haven't used the service, then you probably don't need the subscription.

Minimalism at Your Workplace

(an ideal office with just three chairs and no junk on the table)

The workplace is one of the most important places in anybody's life. The state and condition of this place determines your performance, level of satisfaction and happiness. If you're the owner or manager of a company, you have to carefully choose the location and type of premise that you rent. This is because the workplace will determine the profit that you make.

Generally, a happy and satisfied employee is likely to perform better because he/she can work for longer hours. When thinking of minimalism at work, you have to make sure that you and your employees are happy and comfortable.

You can downsize your life by moving to a smaller office. This way you'll pay less rental charges and hence increase your annual profits. When selecting a new, smaller office, you have to ensure that the amenities within the premise are the same as those in your previous office. This way you can be sure that your (employees) performance won't be affected.

Before you start de-junking and minimalism in the office, you have to consider the number of clients you serve at any one sitting. For instance, you should not move into an office that can accommodate a maximum of three people if you frequently receive more than three people at a go.

(you can have one large multipurpose hall and several small offices)

Instead of having several large offices within the same company, you can decide to rent several small offices and maybe one conference room. The conference room can be used as a spare office, in case one of the employees receives more visitors than his/her office can accommodate.

So as to de-junk and downsize your workplace, you must carefully select the furniture to be placed inside the office. An average office just needs three comfortable chairs and one table. Two of the chairs will be used by visitors while you'll use the third one.

You can also downsize the office by sharing some of the equipment within the same premise. For instance, it is not necessary to have printer in each office. One printer can be positioned centrally in one floor and connected to all the computers. This way anybody can print anything and then go pick it conveniently from the printer. You also don't have to install several Wi-Fi routers within the same building. Rather than do that, just install one powerful router and provide each user with a username and password.

How many desktop/laptop computers do you currently have in your office? If you have more than one, then you need to consider disposing the extra ones and retain just one. Just make sure that the computer has the capacity to handle all the necessary tasks.

So as to downsize your workplace, you should share hot and cold water dispensers. A dispenser can provide up to ten or even twenty liters of water. On the other hand, an average person never drinks more than one liter of water per day while at work. This means that you can never finish the water in the dispenser. Rather than have a dispenser in each office, why not place one in a central location. The water dispenser can serve more than ten people each day (assuming it is refilled each morning.)

You also have to consider getting rid of all the suits in your office and retain only one of them. Since you always go to your home each day, why are you still keeping several suits in the office? They're just occupying space unnecessarily.

You can also de-junk and downsize your office by getting rid of the antiques, trophies and gifts that you've been collecting. Even if you think that they are quite important, the truth is that you don't need them. You should therefore consider disposing them. You can either sell or give them away. You can also decide to place them in the storeroom instead of displaying them on your office table.

To begin the process of de-junking and downsizing your office, you have to go through every square inch of the office and get rid of all the stuff that you don't use. You should go through all the drawers and remove everything that you haven't used for the past couple of months.

What You Must Never Miss When Downsizing Your Life

There are several things that you should never miss when downsizing and de-junking your life. Whether you're moving to a smaller house or office there are minimal standards that you must adhere to. Without some of these things, your life can be very uncomfortable and unsatisfactory.

(never move to a house with no air conditioning system)

Whenever moving to a new property, you must always ensure that the air conditioning is working properly. When compared to large and spacious rooms, smaller rooms require air conditioning so that the occupants don't feel suffocated. You should never move into a new home or office if you're not sure of the state of the air conditioner. Alternatively, you can move to a house with large windows so as to improve the aeration in there. One more advantage of having large windows is that the illumination in the room will be significantly improved.

Even if you'll be using little water, you must ensure that your new home or office has plenty of running water. You must also ensure that the water is safe for consumption.

Unless you're moving to a very remote location, you must ensure that your new home is connected to the national grid. Alternatively, the home can be supplied with reliable electricity from a generator or solar panel. You also have to consider whether a solar water heater is installed in the new home. This is because heating water through electricity or gas is quite expensive. If possible, you should move to a house with solar water heater.

Unlike in the 80s and 90s, it is now almost impossible to survive without reliable internet connection. The internet is quite important because it can be used as a source of information or for entertainment. You can also use the internet to connect with friends or do business. Whenever moving to a new home, you must ensure that there is reliable internet connection.

When downsizing your life by moving to a new house, you must ensure that emergency or precautionary measures have been factored. For instance, the house should have more than one door (just in case of emergency). The home should also have alarms (to deter burglars and robbers) and fire detectors. If possible, ensure that the alarm is designed to notify local emergency response teams automatically when the security is breached.

When de-junking and downsizing your digital life, you should never delete the important files even if you rarely open them. For instance, you shouldn't delete softcopies of your certificates and testimonials. You should also not delete your family photos or those photos that remind you of memorable and interesting events.

Even if you want to completely downsize your life, you should never delete all the music in your PC or phone. If you do so, you'll probably get so bored and download the music once again. However, you can delete music if you have a means of listening to it online.

Instead of selling your stuff instantly you can decide to rent a temporary storage facility and put the stuff in there. Once you realize that you moved something that you can't live without, all you have to do is move it back to your house. After about three months, you'll have figured out what you need and what you don't need in the home. If you haven't needed something that has been lying in the storage facility for the three months, then you probably don't need it. You can therefore go ahead and dispose it.

Conclusion

You have to start the process of downsizing your life as soon as you realize that there is so much going on in your life. No need to keep on postponing your problems. While de-junking and downsizing your life is quite important, you don't have to do it excessively as your life can become very miserable.

When minimizing your life, keep in mind that first impression matters a lot. As soon as somebody sets foot in your home or office, they'll have a rough idea of your character and personality. You therefore have to do everything you can to improve the first impression that you always create. Always ensure that the important stuff isn't missing in your home or office. Can you imagine what will happen if a billionaire investor visits your office and is welcomed into a disorganized office?

You should never rush to minimalism. Take your time to analyze everything in your home or office and decide if you need it or not. You also have to consult your family members before making up your mind on this issue. By downsizing your life, you can easily affect your child's schooling or your partner's convenience when going to work.

So as to minimize your life correctly, just implement the tips listed in this book. Remember that you can use these tips regardless of your current location or career. You can also use these tips to help out a friend who is interested in de-junking and downsizing their live.

Author Bio

Colvin Tonya Nyakundi is a freelance writer and co-author of 'Minimalism: How to De-Junk and Downsize Your Life.' Apart from that book, he has a portfolio of several other publications accumulated in the more than two years that he has been freelancing through www.odesk.com.

He has authored several personal relationships, construction and real estate, lifestyle and travel and holiday guide publications. Other books that he has co-authored include 'How to Survive in the Woods', 'How to Start Making Money Online', 'How to Survive in a Desert', 'How to Improve Your Communication Skills,' 'Construction Guide for New Investors in Real Estate,' 'How to Make Your Backyard a Magnificent Venue for Hosting Events', 'How to Identify the Perfect Holiday Destination', "How Your Favorite Meal Could be Killing You Slowly" and 'How to Prepare and Survive in a Foreign Country.' You can get in touch with him through his official Facebook, tonyanc@facebook.com or follow him on Twitter, @tonyanc.

Check out some of the other JD-Biz Publishing books

Gardening Series on Amazon

Health Learning Series

Amazing Animal Book Series

Learn To Draw Series

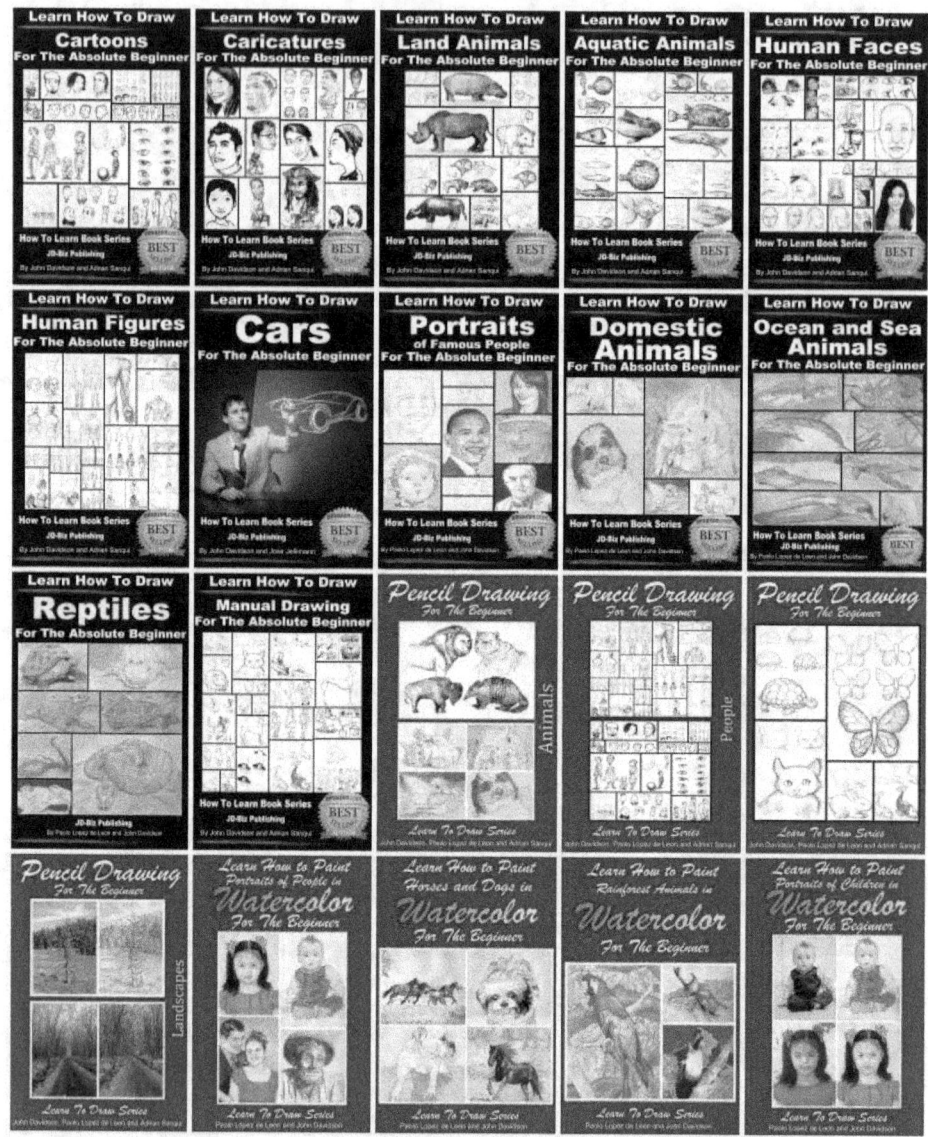

Entrepreneur Book Series

Our books are available at

1. Amazon.com

2. Barnes and Noble

3. Itunes

4. Kobo

5. Smashwords

6. Google Play Books

Publisher

JD-Biz Corp

P O Box 374

Mendon, Utah 84325

http://www.jd-biz.com/

www.ingramcontent.com/pod-product-compliance
Lightning Source LLC
Chambersburg PA
CBHW070507290526
45790CB00003B/1134